the walnut-cracking machine

the walnut-cracking machine

by julie berry

BuschekBooks
Ottawa

Library and Archives Canada Cataloguing in Publication

Berry, Julie
The walnut-cracking machine / Julie Berry.

Poems.
ISBN 978-1-894543-64-4

I. Title.

PS8553.E772W35 2010 C811'.54 C2010-905191-2

Cover image: photograph by Jan Row, used with permission.

Printed in Winnipeg, Manitoba, by Hignell Book Printing.

BuschekBooks, P.O. Box 74053, 5 Beechwood Avenue
Ottawa, Ontario, Canada K1M 2H9
www.buschekbooks.com

BuschekBooks gratefully acknowledges the support of the Canada Council
for the Arts for its publishing program.

**Canada Council
for the Arts**   **Conseil des Arts
du Canada**

this book is for ruth claire berry gifford and macdonald reginald gifford, and in memory of may, reg, eulia and albert

how to tell a good poem

a good poem is built like a rickety platform
attached by a single nail
to the last thing you know

and it's a really good poem
if the nail doesn't hold

contents

brief

my father is a baby
afloat on a thin raft of light
in the upstairs bedroom
his small body steadied
by his mother's hand

he sits in a porcelain basin
in an inch of water

it's summer and my grandmother is alive
she rinses soap off my father's shoulder
with the water from her cupped hand

they don't know about me

hairpin stories

hairpin turns hairpin excursions
hairpin fishing rods carried by hairpin boys
who traverse the rivers and vales of my bent knees
i hop them up and down
up and down the mountains

mornings we teach my baby sister
to tie perfect bows on her playpen
drop her from impossible
heights watch
her bounce
boing
boing
on the couch

visit

here is what you must take
a small suitcase full of the unexpected
lightning/rain
half-grown barley/elderberries
mad dogs/tomato worms
leave your cringes
your walking on ice

after you finish unpacking
slide the suitcase under the bed

the bed is for circumnavigating
afternoon naps, for sailing across
the crocheted tussle of deep water
and skirting the flat islands on your tummy
to drift to delight from skirmish to skirmish
while nasty pirates make you helpless
with ropes and ribbon

daguerreotypes

it's best to go alone
anyway your little sister likes it better farther west
with aunt nelly and the cows
the chickens and the cousins

aunt iva is *your* favourite
she oversees your eye exercises at bedtime
before you turn out the light, insists you chew
each mouthful a certain number of times
breakfast
lunch
dinner

evenings she organizes her stamps and coins
on the gate leg table while you play the game
she taught you solitaire in the secret shadow
forest of walnut legs

you are the only one who remembers the blocks
in the wooden box behind the stove
the blocks with faces you arranged
on the parlour floor

small houses and fenced gardens
with the faces of mothers and fathers
children too blurred to recognize or too long dead
a smiling dog with a plumed tail keeps watch at night

going up north in the cold war

i was well-travelled for my age
peed my snowsuit in hamilton
discovered the correlation between chicory
                         grasshoppers and air travel in malton
learned the difference between a hill and a mountain
in humber summit
was intimate with the niagara gorge
rode a farting workhorse up the scotch road
                              to sandy york's dad's farm
glimpsed lake erie from the far end of bessie
saw a crippled boy up close at the fingal public school
coveted the twirling skirts of the grade one girls in little italy
where our teacher taught us all to repeat after her
          riposati e e vai a dormire

but this is about going up north to a cottage on an island
in lake nipissing and here is what i remember:

you had to go by boat for the last part of the trip

my father kept us on our toes all the way up highway 11
by exclaiming about the indians he spotted in the trees
and ditches beside the highway
                         by bolton
everybody knew he was kidding except jane
who leapt from one side of the back seat to the other all the way there
this was before seatbelts or the sardine incident

sit back for christ's sake sit back said our mother from time to time

when we got to our island
the smell of pine needles in hot july sun
                              settled deep inside me
and would be a prelude to every paradise thereafter

my twenty-something mother held the screen door open for us
and while she put the groceries away she warned us about the bears
we didn't find out about the watersnakes until later
but the whole week was worry-free for me because
according to my calculations
our island was beyond the reach of nuclear missiles

sugarfoot girl

from the basement of the dirty yellow brick three-story walk-up
across the rexdale ugliness of dried grass and spent sidewalk
sugarfoot girl executes a dazzling leap over the ornamental fence
and skitters through the library doors into the tall-windowed glade
carries the wilderness of wagon train of river-fording sunburned days
across the shining floors two steps down into the sun-riffled air
to the bottom of the world to the beginning of where she is going
and opens it on her lap

from the shelf of the blue fairy red fairy green fairy
up kipling ave to islington
past molson's brewery
                  the steinburg water tower
two hours on the 401
in the smoke-filled back seat of a tin car with no seatbelts to the

gully

mornings the words that are in her
pool at the ends of her fingers and

gully

the hidden springs
and unexpected mud
the specific attitudes of beech
trees wild
ginger and light

go down there i'll say

i know about mourning doves waterstriders skunk cabbage
last year's milkweed madness desire hopelessness
anger appeasement control and power
the sloppy nest-building and unexpected brilliance of doves
the way waterstriders let other waterstriders know
by beating on the skin of the stream
$\qquad\qquad\qquad\qquad\qquad\qquad\qquad$ when they are ready for sex

i am interested in the hooked beaks
of skunk cabbage in late winter the way they poke their purple
noses out of the earth along creek beds and in swampy places

i wonder about the dark grey of the milkweed stands
beside the creek where i have never seen them before

when i am old and white-haired
riding along the scotch road
hunched up in the back seat of somebody else's car
i'll tap my bony finger against the window
$\qquad\qquad\qquad\qquad\qquad\qquad\qquad$ go down there i'll say
past the trees that line the north edge of that field
go in late april and you will find the first marsh marigolds
go in mid-april with a shovel
$\qquad\qquad\qquad\qquad$ dig wild leeks
make yourself a cheese and leek sandwich

stand anywhere in the gully on a warm night in mid-may
if you're lucky you'll hear the rustle of may apples
trilliums and maidenhair fern unfurling under last year's leaves
you will think a million mice are running through the woods
$\qquad\qquad\qquad\qquad\qquad\qquad\qquad$ around your feet
$\qquad\qquad\qquad\qquad$ between your legs
$\qquad$ it'll give you the willies

i will be known for my knowledge of the gully
it will be said nobody knew the gully better than julie

birthplace

lie down with me on this old road in spring
and enter the penumbra of may apples

farther on is the birthplace of the gully
where the field loses and finds its life
and there are no roads
from centuries of suns and moons and rainy days
the world seeps into itself and is swallowed
by the continual trickle of its own run-off

i'll take you there if you like
we'll snap the small twigs we carried
so far for no reason
follow deer along the gentle fall of land
where fields give way to entanglements
of wild cucumber
stinging nettle and poison hemlock
we won't be able to see
our feet we'll lose sight
of our bodies
and each other

in these parts fringed gentian are rare

i come upon them in the shadow
of the collapsing bank
along a ruined road
that once joined the scotch road to fingal
at the bottom of each blossom
a golden coin

here you will find a hillside of periwinkle
the foundation of a burned barn
and the last home of my great-grandmother
back door open wide
hanging by a single hinge over garbage flung
by long-gone neighbours

a stove struggles against the downward spill
an upside-down baby carriage

my father pulled the swing bridge down when he was a boy not much
left now a few stories a brother lost and found then lost again in the un-
expected february runoff a plastic bouquet of daffodils shoved into the
dirt beside the freshly backhoed valley the grapevine house its graceful
under-scheme of apple tree gone the fragments of blue willow buried
among arrowheads and aluminum saucepans the glacial riff of these
footloose gullies and fields

the names of everything in you

when my uncle flattens the grapevine house with his backhoe
and the furniture salesman and his wife who are dying of bingo
drag their thirty-two foot trailer down there
and park it in the middle of what used to be
my personal garden of sumac and purple phlox
not to mention bury two of their cats
run over by the same truck on different days
i have no choice but to move on

gully
        i will never forget you
anchored to my childhood
by the old stove
                        half-buried between the sumacs
and carrion flower vines tripping over themselves
crazy to conquer the fencerows

and gully
i have learned the names of everything in you

concerning mr ambrose

mr ambrose ran the nursery down the road
grew trees and bushes mainly
no flowers that i recall   he had one hand
and a hook where the other hand should have been
he could trim a bush efficiently
i liked to watch him do it
there was a touch of horror
to the watching which i enjoyed

he's dead now but just yesterday i thought of him as i passed the place
his nursery used to be and i wondered did they bury the hook with him
and isn't it strange to think of his bones and his hook lying there in the dark
coffin and finally just
                the hook

why it's important to wake up from your dreams

we are fastened to our dreams securely as gulliver was tied to lilliputia
with thousands of flimsy strings only it's more scientific the law of attraction
and repulsion those magnetic forces the north and south poles (let us not
forget the way iron filings arrange themselves on a clean sheet of paper)
                    and everyone knows
                            invisibility is no argument for non-existence

of course there is no denying our dreams are susceptible to gravity
and magnetic forces of course they fall to earth not unlike rain
and of course they disappear down deep cracks and end up very far down
                          where the creatures with bums for heads live

if you think the earth does not feed on dreams you are mistaken
without dreams earth would sicken and die and since the dreamer
is attached to the dream (see above) she is in danger
of being caught in the rush the headlong stream and dragged along

                          the mysteries are thick down there
thicker even than here on the surface where the blessed may choose to stand
upright and listen for minutes at a time to the sound a single leaf makes
as it blows across the pavement at night
                    which is why it's important to wake up
                            from your dreams

why it's important to remember your dreams

dreams are either remembered or forgotten and both kinds of dreams
exist as large bodies of water exist except the one near where you live
is the one you swim in frequently and this lake (let's call it erie)
is like the dreams you remember and you dry off after swims in it
sit beside it for hours
listen to its rhythmic shh shh shh

                                 or you think of its violence
when you're safe at home on stormy days
because friends of friends have drowned in it and in winter you marvel
at its solid state its frozen swells
but you are never dressed warmly enough to stay as long as you'd like
                                               you can travel
to the other side of the earth but the body of water you live near
and the dreams you remember are with you always
and may well be a source of continual personal growth
and understanding if you can afford a good dream therapist
                                       and/or swimming instructor

those dreams you never remembered but dreamed all the same
or remembered in the morning and never thought of again
                                       those dreams
are like a lake on another continent you may never visit
but even though they're somewhere else they're still evaporating
forming clouds and raining down on you interrupting picnics
spoiling outings turning the air of spring mornings wet and green
or gathering strength somewhere getting big enough to be seen
from a satellite to be tracked and named you will have to find
your umbrella crisscross your picture window with masking tape

hunker down

mount vesuvius with lips

i loved your white rain downspout hairwashing
like the black and white mother on tv you were
always in another room getting ready to blow
mount vesuvius with lips of red hair shiny
as the coal under the railroad bridge next door
never ever go there you said while soot settled
on the windowsills we pressed and cajoled
the orange-eyed margarine bags into a spreadable consistency
you and dad tossed them from the doorway of the kitchen
across the living room back and forth over jackie's playpen

how strange and faraway you seem now
and would have seemed then if i had known
what mothers are capable of your cigarettes burned
slim brown stains on the edges of everything
                              i always knew where you had been

the summer of sponge baths at the kitchen sink
long hot visits to the beach the night you said
your love affair was just another reason to feel
guilty our father cried a little his mother his brother
running up the grassy slope to the house
our grandfather idling outside in the pick-up

you must
have been
so lonely

you scare me mom more than nuclear war
or the inevitability of carcinogens
                              you scare me so much
my shoes fly off my father's shoes fly off
the car overturned in a ditch outside of town
and me waking up without a scratch among the unearthly
undulations of a let-go raspberry patch

erosion

the land washed away
so slowly she hardly noticed
she had taken the snug safe earth
                              for granted
waves, their wistful soothe
in and out

under her bark
small bugs nibbled
and her clear sap always
moving from the dark
to the light and back again

a slow sliding collapse
at the end of a very wet spring
left her sideways for a decade

now she is all things gone
an old photo of eleven people
dead their children and their children's
children the hospital where she was born
now a vacant lot at the corner of pearl
                              and curtis
the cottage bakery, 311 talbot
                        gone
broke   absolutely
everything must go

parade

after he went blind
i'd watch my grandfather shave
he'd forget i was there
press hard with the shaver and afterwards
rub and rub his cheek   his chin
i could see the feel of his smooth flesh
pleased him

i seldom cry
this dry-eyed splendour i inherited
from my grandmother
i never saw her cry
not even when her sisters died or her brother
her sister jennie left behind a cardboard box
full of yellowed flannel nightgowns
in the only photograph i've ever seen of her
a silo a barn and two cows are tangled in her hair
iva was the one i knew best
a porch smelling of narcissus
and something else i never figured out
raccoon-skin rugs
jar rings sewn on the bottom so they wouldn't slip
sweet william the pansies the grapevines
and grapes   honest-to-god   grapes
growing so close to the house
                              you could lean back
in your chair and pick them out the parlour window

her brother ingersoll left this world
unappreciated as may apples
ghost-like in august shade
he kneeled
reached under a green umbrella
offered me the only one i've ever tasted

a horse being let out of the barn after a long winter
made my grandmother run out her upstairs window
i thought i was downstairs she tells us
i love to see her falling in her little dress falling
to the garden into the hollyhocks
                                        the nasturtiums
                                                tumbling
a wrapped candy tossed into the road

come winter

driving down to the farm something's changed
the birds are only birds now
the sky behind them smudged
someone with dirty fingers reached for them and missed
they fly around me like always
but they don't talk to me
why is that   they've always called out before
wherever i was
risk everything
risk it   risk it

when i get to the farm there are twenty or more old boxes stacked up
under the plum trees old banana boxes full of receipts and cash register
tapes rolled into neat bundles with elastic bands you gotta keep them
for a certain number of years for the income tax says grandpa there's
two big holes dug in the back lawn grandma tells me the septic tank's
not working grandpa's dumping the pail out back just like the old days

we go sit in what used to be the parlour but now it's their bedroom
i was just upstairs yesterday says grandma and made it airtight but
when i told your aunt shirley you shoulda heard her she says i can't
go upstairs anymore says i'll break my hip all over again it doesn't
feel right sleeping downstairs she shakes her head i've slept upstairs
all my life

grandpa changes the subject he's heard a rumour the government's
going to cut off the old age pension if they do that there'll be frozen
bodies all over the place come winter he says you won't be able to
walk down the street without tripping over them thank god i'll be
dead soon he says i always knew it'd get this bad

otherwise known as mandrake

in may at the end
of winter's holding
this umbrella's poison
begins unfolding

one flower, seven
petals waxen-white
easily missed by folks
with city-sight

blossoms in the shade
of self-made gloom
through the earliest days
of light-filled june

young ones who eat the root
have been known to die
grownups may hallucinate
and die, or prophesy

its fruit swells
to the size of a plum
first solid as a stone
then softening some

through july it ripens
from shiny and green
to a subtle yellow-white
the colour of cream

some say when it's soft
it can be consumed
others claim to eat it
means certain doom

i tasted one
it was sweet and good
but i leave it to you
as to whether *you* should

my grandfather died in the tim hortons parking lot

cherry pie half-eaten on the dash no doubt his spirit rose
quickly and he looked down on his daughter his wife
as they kneeled over his body saw their hands like birds
fluttering over his frightened heart crashing crashing
into windows like a trapped starling when he died the air
over our town swelled with music from the old time gospel hour
                              and the trestle over sunset trembled

from up there he saw the old ford stir up years of dust
along the back concessions while he delivered the mail
for hazel and roy or sweet corn and strawberries
to palmers' red and white in shedden

                              bush road coon road lake road scotch
stacey's jones's the root sisters goldie and emerson cryan from up there
the row of norway spruce receded and the rogue spring trickled harmlessly
down the lane into waist-high jewelweed he loved everything then
the fine sand of the laneway the smell of pineapple weed in summer
basin of warm water on the back porch cake of soap floating
rows of tobacco picked leaf by leaf tied onto slats
                              cured to gold in the red insul-brick kiln

in the dark winter-shack under the pear tree he bundled
the velvet leaves into bales weighed them got them ready
for the auction o he did he did love everything then
even the horse that kicked him that set his tea quivering
                              in a thousand delicate saucers

between

the spring he died
my grandfather planted corn and peas
in a garden he dug within the cement foundation
of the last of the disappearing barns

there's a photograph

one seed at rest
in the air between
his hand and the furrow
he made with the heel of his boot
one seed between earth
and his cupped hand

the walnut-cracking machine

aunt nelly was a fitch from fingal
small like a wren
inside her she carried
an immense drawstring bag
crammed with small kindnesses
her husband ingersoll was well-read
a farmer with a butterfly collection
and a killing jar he kept on the kitchen counter
he was born and died in the same house
painted once as high as he could reach
without a ladder

late april snow covered the green grass
the morning i dropped in for tea
a vise-like creation sat on the kitchen table
somebody had been using it to crack walnuts
i tried it out a few times
while aunt nelly boiled water
fussed with a plate of cookies
uncle ingersoll called from the dining room
would you like to see the automatic nut cracker?

he was using a walker so the trip through the kitchen
down the back porch steps
across the wet lawn took a good half hour
the walnut cracker had been out all winter
he kneeled
tinkered with it a few minutes
nelly yelled from the back door
it'll never work

he reached for the switch
nothing
plug it in he yelled to nelly
i took a step back
alarmed that electricity was involved

32

it started up right away
people miles away that morning
in shedden or frome
planting peas or leaf lettuce
likely straightened their backs
turned their faces to the southwest

but when uncle ingersoll dumped
the pail of last fall's walnuts
into the large funnel-shaped pipe
the trees the house the clouds
the planets and all their moons
collapsed under the weight of the din
all creation tumbled together down the pipe
and cracked in a rupturous clatter
i pressed the heels of my hands over my ears
and squeezed my eyes shut

the machine broke up the shells
spit them out one side
the meat of the walnuts dropped into
a small china bowl underneath

uncle ingersoll reached down
turned the machine off
the silence was a solid embraceable thing
i carried home
sometimes i take it out and hold it
and dream of someday making something
as loud and useful
as the walnut-cracking machine

little strip room in heaven

in the night my grandmother calls for help
she's stuck somewhere in heaven
it takes me forever to dress
my shoes are nowhere to be found
so i go without
from the top of the biggest beech in the woods
it's a short leap
to the little strip room in heaven

so this is where grandma is spending eternity
in a small shack with a ceiling so low it rubs
against the pom-pom of her toque
soft gold leaves on the strip room table
the scent of cured tobacco in her hair

my grandmother is stuck
beside her husband in the strip room
where they sort and grade tobacco leaves
through november

december

the fire burns down

by christmas every velvet
leaf has been touched twice

where would you rather be
i ask

flora

saturday

in theory   explains rob   she has no brain
under the delicate umbrella of my surprise
he clarifies   no cerebrum

in theory   i ask

well   he says
we think she knows some things
that take some kind of a brain

he lifts flora from the table in the kitchen
where she spends her days
it's dinner time
jen shakes the checkered cloth
out over the table
                    smooths it

the longest we've been away   says rob
was a week and we missed her so much
we came back a week early

i set the table while jen makes gravy
tells about the tests the doctors did to find out
why flora doesn't have a brain

nobody   she says
really knows

sunday

dawn   mid-february
i say good-bye and head to my car
the snowmen in the backyard
are melting in rain

i'm miles south before i realize
thieves have smashed my coffee mug
stolen my pound of teeswater cheese

that night i dream a bride
has baked a pig-shaped cake for her husband
she writes the things she needs in icing
but the words are spelled wrong

    shoos   *furnicher*

the father of the bride points to his wife
who sits in the cab of a pickup at the side of the road
she won't go out in the boat with me anymore
                              he complains

her hands are out of sight
and her arms make small jerking movements
i think perhaps she's knitting

or loading a pistol

i wonder what flora dreams

monday

my friend calls at 7 a.m. to cancel dinner tells me her dream
about a woman who keeps her brain wrapped up in the fridge
like christmas cake and i tell her how i heard about a man
who dreamed of a world where everybody eats their
own body parts how in his dream he watched himself
reach up into his skull with a long spoon and eat his brain
looking more and more imbecilic with every mouthful

                  today at cut and paste
we're making big paper faces shaped like hearts
philip's heart-nose has fallen off
he asks me to put it back on in a better place
it keeps sticking to my tongue   he explains
and my mouth won't open

sarah shrieks
          my head
i can't find my head

have you looked on the floor   i ask
she crawls under the table
it's not here teacher   she starts to cry
i spot it stuck to the seat of her pants
pull it off and hand it back to her

tuesday

it's valentine's day
so we're talking about hearts
make a fist everybody
that's how big your heart is   i say
eric points to a place at the back of his head
there's place in your head where if you fall
and break it you die

my grandpa died says steph
his bones are in a box under our feet
the kids look down
in one synchronised instant
they all lift their feet off the floor

you need a heart to live   i add
but i don't tell them they could
live without a brain

wednesday

fog

       snow

             mud

february inhales

                 sucks us in

dream neil is misbehaving *again*
when i pick him up
             he shrinks
suddenly i'm holding a little boy
between my thumb and forefinger

at school erin tells me she's afraid of earthquakes
she's making a heart-shaped book
these are earthquake lines she tells me
they're all wiggly because of the shaking
at night i can't sleep in my bed   she says
because of the earthquakes
so my mom sleeps in one chair
and i sleep in the other

thursday to sunday

i get the flu
the parts of me that don't hurt are so irrelevant
they disappear
though my shadow surprises me often

its completeness

in the gullies and on hillsides
north of lake erie
the snow grows wings
flies into fields farther west
a cardinal sharpens his song
on the blue edge of these late winter days
while the lake ice sews itself to the shore
in long loopy stitches

last week when i held flora in my arms
she clutched at the air
quivered like a small engine

monday

it's career week in kindergarten
what are you going to be   i ask the kids
kristine who hates barbie dolls is going to be a movie star
a teacher and a pet store owner
brandon thinks he'll be a pet store owner too
only i'm just going to have iguanas
and turtles at my store   he tells us
nicky wants to be a bird and michelle a mermaid
keaton wants to be a father

it's over a week since i held flora
felt her body stiffen   her distress
at being held by a stranger

tuesday

first warm day of the year
pink and purple winter coats are piled on the sidewalk
some of the girls prance and leap across the soggy grass
i'm a lost baby horse   says tracy
she curls up beside the fence
makes heartrending whinny-sounds in her throat
half a dozen mommy horses gallop to the rescue
a pastel blur of tossing manes
                                        flicking their tails
pawing the ground with their delicate boots

andrew's watching with me

he moves closer
                        speaks in a low voice
i'm not going to be nothing when i grow up
what do you mean   i ask

he studies his feet
my dad comed out of my one grandma
and my mom comed out of my other grandma
but i comed out of *my* mom   he looks at me
as if this fact explains every sadness there ever was
when he sees my confusion he adds
it's fake   teacher   it's fake

i still don't get it and he's looking like he's sorry
he ever brought it up

o flora dear
can there ever be a *gentle*
gentle enough for you

we're holding off on the stomach tube   says rob
as long as possible
eating is one of the few things she does

he and jen share the irony—
or is it sadness

          or pain—
with me
like a crust of necessary bread

a little dutch boy made of plaster
hangs in the kitchen
on the wall above flora's table

the blue of his cap
his purposeful stride
his cheerful wooden shoes

he used to hang in my mother's kitchen
says jen
and i always loved him

small poem

i discovered an owl pellet
at the base of the white pine
the greyest thing
i have ever seen
the grey
of solid dust

inside i found
the femur of a small animal
its skull
teeth
tiny claws

strange
i remembered it
as heavy to my friend
when in fact
it was far lighter
in my hand
than i had expected

three heavens

in my grandfather's heaven the radio plays night and day
how great thou art the old rugged cross in his hands a rich
sandy loam the clay clods gone   earth anywhere he picks it up
runs through his fingers like silk scarves the smell of quack grass
surprises him for eternity like cinnamon without the bitterness
rain falls when needed straight-down drenchings no hailstorms
no droughts and every night the corn-loving raccoons are treed
in the maples and beeches along the creek hound dogs
                                                at the bottom of every one

in uncle ingersoll's heaven the middle of the night has settled
forever over the hills near talbot creek where shattered stones
give off an ancient smell like the air before fish and ingersoll
knows back home the kitchen is dark though the freshly-wiped
counters shine and nelly's asleep in their bedroom off the parlour
the chinese walnut he transplanted from the dead colonel's land
has grown tall enough to fringe the house the horseshoe pit
in delicate moony shadow and by day a never-ending line
of small appliances limp up the laneway in need of salvation
the lost tools found and sumac grows thick enough for candlesticks

aunt nelly's heaven is in the linen department of zeller's
with everything 50% off the house is painted all the way to the top
the barn doesn't blow over the sugar bush is spared in the ice storm
of '76 the front porch in aunt nelly's heaven is a sunny well-used
room with every national geographic since 1936 shelved in perfect
order somewhere else   she has a garden of fat wormless cabbages
nasturtiums up to her knees and the sidewise glances of dark-eyed birds
exude a certain perfect melancholy as they set out across the soybean sea

empire

he knew how things were going to turn out for everyone
one july morning he was trimming lettuce when
a truck from georgia pulled up in front

lazy assholes he occasionally said of the help
we made a line and unloaded a thousand watermelons one by one
they couldn't work fast if their lives depended on it
he whispered to me

but their lives did not depend on it
one would become an accountant
and another would become a drunk
keep this to yourself
he warned me

morning in white's bush

when i looked back at my bed last night says jane
it was a blossom
the quilt looked like the sepals
and the sheets were all foofy like petals
downstairs in the kitchen the peaches were glowing
like a bowl of suns
and when i stepped outside the night wore
a veil of song
                    only it wasn't crickets
it was stars
much zingier than crickets we agree
i've noticed says jane that things come in clumps

crows make a sudden
puckering of the morning
pinch here
tuck there
the light knows nothing i say
and jane agrees
draws it in around her
like a shawl

we need to read this book without an introduction
jane believes or an afterward
who cares if the writer was a child or an adult
it's all extraordinary and beautiful nonetheless
and what is mental illness really says jane
when you get old or crazy
words and events slide off their meanings
habits and memories settle slightly skewed
you need someone to remind you
                    of the simplest things

the angel-maker's mother

there's nowhere without them said jane
everything has its own angel she said
and she lent me the book to prove it
pansies sweet william the giant willow
in her back yard the stones in her driveway
look a little to the right and up she told me

that summer i brought two angels home
from england rolled up in my bag
but i got tired of them watching me in the stairwells
    ascending
descending
they're in the attic now

years later i met the man from the dream desert
who makes the angel moulds
as a teenager he drove his parents crazy
his greasy fingers the way he hunched over
his plate his disregard for social conventions
he eventually got his papers in tool and dye
bought a little place outside lawrence station
people think angels are lighter than air he says
but really they're heavy
              drop one in a pond
                    it'll sink like a stone
he winks at me

the angel-maker's mother will tell you
as a child he fell into fires
ran head-on into picnic tables garages
split his head open countless times
broke his collar bone   wrist   arm
has a scar under his nose
a metal plate in his ankle

she swears he was too heavy for this world
that night he couldn't sleep
she noticed something moving under his skin
he told her the angels were waiting for him
and she looked out the window
but they had gone
leaving the air wrinkled as bedclothes

the first boy ever

bats fly out from under the eaves
into the chaos of everything
here i am here i am cries the boy
the leaves of white ash shield the rusted
remains of his grandfather's buick le sabre
from the darkening sky

he climbs in
turns the key
sumac busts out from under the hood
its green fire power igniting
the combustible maroon fruit

the woods   everything
                    jumps

sunk hub-deep in queen anne's lace
he spins his tires
lurches out and steers through raspberry loop-de-loops
over the hill
down to the creek without a name

like a bat
he sees
        through sound
the colours of things

has felt blue like a soft breeze
caress the back of his raised hand
has endured that red throb in his temple
that pinch of yellow
sting of fuchsia

this green ocean will one day wash over him
the inexorable undertow of madness will drag him out to sea

he says to his mother
that he wants to be
the first boy ever

why can't i be he asks

pigweed story

who threw the dinner plates into the field
and who in the world ploughed them under
every spring sharp bits of blue willow rise
to the surface of the freshly-harrowed earth
which always reminds me of a story from china
how the freshly-made sky cracked up
and pieces fell to the ground
i can never resist picking them up

one evening
pockets saggy and dangerous
i cross the cornfield where the house i believe in used to stand
weave through a fencerow thick with sumac
find martha in the spelt pulling pigweed

just back from england she tells me she saw
buckingham palace and st peter's
toured westminster abby
i went there once i tell her
i walked on wordsworth
we laugh and pull out pigweed
pigweed pigweed
and more pigweed
until the sun goes down

some kind of immense indiscernible shift is going on in the world

bermuda is known to have slid out from under wyoming years ago i am
a teacher i teach the rocky mountains draw cross-sections on the blackboard
which is flat and black and comes from ordovician guck the bilateral
spreading of the ocean floor has always excited me i know uplifting
accelerates erosion and because the atlantic is spread wide europe
will probably never hit you in nevada still you can never be sure
look at bermuda—warm and pink under kansas one minute—
                                        under yakutat alaska the next

i sit in the vinyl chair with wooden arms on 2A the ward where my son
spent christmas and where he will spend his twenty-first birthday
with hortense bird chuckie phillip and smoothy some with privileges
some without i watch diehard with hortense   my son and the others
wander in and out it's hortense's favourite something big like bermuda
moves deep beneath the hospital something big and memorable
like the first of my father's convertibles

i visit my son every day my mother has a car says phillip
when i pass him in the hall up on 2A my mother's not a seamstress
he tells everyone i watch my son play solitaire in the empty tv room
chuckie shouts musically from a locked side room i want to
f------u-----c-----k you i want to f----u----c----k you
i want to f---u----c----k you and your mother and your grandmother
i want to f------u-----c-----k you he bangs bangs bangs on the door
of the room where they put you if you're a danger to yourself or others
after a few weeks i notice i have begun to talk like phillip
that friendly newsy way he tells you things my mother has
                                        a car she is not a seamstress

it's true our minds began to leap and boil one sunny day in the pleistocene
worms turn into butterflies bats see with their ears some young men
go mad in the prime of their youth and other young men do not
if pennsylvania collides with utah if a new ocean forms east of california
and west of the grand canyon and the continent of north america
tips and slides under the atlantic we'll sing all of us who know
something about madness we'll sing and sing and sing until hawks
cliff erodes into lake erie proving aunt jane right and finally after
all those red-haired years of never wearing pink and never being
the tallest or the fastest hortense bird recently widowed will pose
like a goddess for the men who never wanted her in 1977

another more sensible heaven

the heaven of my son is a detailed and complicated
sketch revised moment to moment its inhabitants laugh
like crazy or weep with desolation at the drop of a hat
and they are all willing to crawl under any piece
of furniture to comfort a friend or a stranger

there's no such thing as normal in my son's heaven no
pills or needles or locked rooms everyone loves him
and listens to him making sense is unheard of
and if anybody suggests it they are sent packing
to another more sensible heaven

moon river

the last time our family was whole
was the august of the total lunar eclipse
we were camped on a cliff
my husband and i
and our four sons
at the sandhills

the night of the eclipse
i was in love with another man
not my husband

i apologized for this
years later after the marriage was over
after enough pain had passed under the bridge
to carry the whole thing off
downstream somewhere
it was a real apology
i really was sorry

not that the marriage was over
but that i had been unfaithful
and so oblivious to my husband's pain
my ex-husband's pain

but i was speaking
of the eclipse

we took a blanket to the highest point of land
watched the moon move slow as an hour hand
into our shadow

watched it turn from an empty white dish
into a coppery plum
an immense motionless sphere
over lake erie

it was a warm night
the leaves of the trembling aspens
along the ridge
shone not
stirred not

i wish
i could say i saw moon river
grow thin that night
that i noticed its silver path
go out like a light
but all i remember
is the moon itself
how round and sweet
and delicious it looked
in the palm of my hand

i plan to be cremated

but when i look down at my hands i vacillate
hate the thought of them being reduced to ashes
hands ought to be preserved
they have done so much
if my hands must be burned up and turned into ashes
let them be burned in a small oven
separate from the rest of my body
let them be sprinkled under the young beech tree
perched at the very tip of the finger of land
that juts into the gully behind my grandfather's farm

no   not sprinkled
i don't want the ashes of my hands
to blow out into the swampy parts
where the skunk cabbage breed and die
i want someone to use a small trowel
to bury them in a hole beside the young beech
so something of my hands will move up
into the new leaves each spring

get rained on
consume light
fall

variations on swimming

dog barks on the fifth night of the heat wave and the fan
swooshes me downstairs out the door
into air that feels like watermelon out of the fridge
                                        cool delicious surprise

off the back step i dive
a shallow dive
to avoid the lawn furniture
paddle over the fence
out the neighbour's driveway
east on wellington

at forest i switch to a sloppy front crawl
before long i'm treading water in the stagnant
headwaters at first and talbot
where a malignant mass of box stores
have replaced the city golf course

the night after the earth movers scraped all day
to make way for parking lots i waded through
the still warm bleed of dirt to the single old lilac bush
left standing by the doomed clubhouse
clearly it was the lilac's last hours
                                so i broke off a few limbs
no measly sprigs of blossoms for a tumbler
to set on the kitchen window sill
i should have had an axe or a saw
each branch was as tall as me
the size around of a child's wrist
i gnawed off the last stubborn strings of bark

back home i smiled at my image in the bathroom mirror
triumphant woman-face aglow
nestled in mauve and green lilac-confusion

then i noticed something written on the mirror
in soap letters
            fuck you mom

when i was nineteen i was taught drownproofing
at the university of waterloo the instructors analysed
my kick using newton's laws
filmed my legs from underwater windows
so i could see where i was going wrong
back then you needed to stay afloat
for a certain number of minutes in order to graduate

two summers later when my first son was born
i dreamed a dark monster pulled me under
three more sons and so it was i learned
to breathe underwater
to read the words
                    fuck you mom
on the bathroom mirror

and laugh

celebration

your sam-girl would like to confess
she stole chocolate peanut clusters
out of the lori sweet boxes
and sneaked into the staff washroom
to kiss the hired help

another thing you don't know:
she burrowed into the meat of your laugh
the same laugh that disarmed the customers
in the confusion of your blooming hilarity
they'd lose their sadnesses
and on the way out they'd
pat their pockets absentmindedly
feeling for the heaviness they'd misplaced

you smelled of oranges and celery at my graduation
could trim a case of iceburg lettuce in twelve minutes
legions of black-handled knives were stored out back
in empty ice cream containers

o the trips you made
with the bleeding help
to and from emerg

work from dawn to dust
you told your daughters

today's your seventy-fifth birthday
the golf cart is parked alongside
your brand new poodle-dog and the
hummingbird feeders are full

remember lucretius

i teach whole numbers and decimals through september
the proper way to read them don't blame me if what i teach
you turns out to be wrong i tell them lucretius said the moon
was the size of his thumb and so it was for generations

after lunch it's social studies the first people came
to north america across the bering land bridge i tell them
they write it down but remember lucretius i say
                                        and hold up my thumb

some of the children have left early for thanksgiving
here in ontario officials are giving speeches about the lack
of available vaccines in the eventuality of biological terrorism
it's 3:28 i'm holding them in the doorway waiting for the bell
lisa says she heard one thing about easter and then another
so she's not sure who to believe

i always thought it was about this man who died on a cross
but david says that's not what it's about the children crowd
in the doorway they just want to go home i try to clear up lisa's
confusion tell her the man did die on the cross on a friday
and on sunday people say he came back to life and went up
to god his father in heaven the bell rings and in seconds
                                        everyone's gone

to be the teacher

i walk to school along the swooping sidewalk cross
the interrupted gully strewn with paper cups chip bags
pass the same gardens every day i have never stopped
wondering what it is to be the teacher to call a mother
and tell her that her son has tipped over is spilling his
goodness in the vacant lot between the arena and the
strip club he's breathing like a fresh-caught fish i want
to say gasping for the town he swam in yesterday
from arson to jaywalking to crying at the drop
of a hat to swearing and the very next day he's
building a plywood model of john cabot's matthew
with sails cut from an old t-shirt

in september i learn their names with pleasure
the way i learn the weeds along the back laneways
candice kayla mike and michael the difference
between them as big as hershel's universe and the
view of his sister's poor broken foot i observe them
like a naturalist notes the first flowers before the trees
get their leaves before june before the cow parsnips
and wild cucumbers take over

i have my own key to the school and other keys
to cupboards and closets jammed with old bunson
burners and test tubes pencils chalk
paper i can go even deeper down through
the door in john's room that says 'no admittance
to teaching staff' down down the metal stairs
i open the steel door everything i don't need
                                    is stored here

a quiet boy named thomas finds a low cupboard
under the stage when he is putting away the gym mats
and i think of it for days i'm looking for a place
to spy on the school to watch from a hidden place
close up i dream of crawling in some morning
of pulling the door closed behind me i want to hear
the school breathe hear the teachers rush to assemble
the necessary materials before the bell i want to hear
the children hurry into their classrooms before
announcements attendance o canada i want
to listen in that silence before the teaching begins

worse than jesus christ

ben's head is flat at the back he says jesus christ out on the schoolyard
and because he knows i'm close enough to hear him i have to tell him
he's not allowed to say jesus christ
                           minutes before in the teacher's
staff room mrs poulton told me the head of the united church should
resign because he said jesus christ might not actually have been
the son of god per se the bell rang so i couldn't ask her if she knew
jesus was sitting on her lap just then like a ventriloquist's dummy
he turned his wooden head slowly took in the room his mouth
opened and closed but don't ask me who was doing the talking

mrs poulton ben and i have something in common it's like
the holy trinity i don't get it but i know it's important i'm pretty
religious i've seen the angel gabriel walk over a hill back behind
my grandfather's farm he was blonde and a golden light shone
around him once i picked up a small angel at the foot of a beech
tree and watched him shrink to nothing in the palm of my hand

i don't know why ben's head is flat he's one of eight born
to a migrant farm family maybe it's because his mother was bent
over picking cucumbers or tomatoes for the entire pregnancy or
maybe he lay on his back for too long while his mother helped
with the tobacco crop and kept his brothers and sisters from being run
over by the tractor or falling into the irrigation pond
                                  his eyes
are blue with lashes that curve so long and dark they cast fringed
shadows across a room i don't know what he sees with those beautiful
eyes i think he was happy once somewhere else maybe under some
sumacs in a weedy hedgerow he was long gone by the time i met him
and nobody knew what to do with him we suspended him every chance
we got it was easy he refused to do as he was told and he often said
worse than jesus christ right to our faces

night school

the first night my class is seated in a field of teasel and mullein
i have prepared a last minute lesson about floods
rivers over-run their banks i try to tell them
people sit on their rooftops waiting for rescue boats
but the kids aren't settling
the kids aren't settling
they are *never* settling down

the next night a boy with the mind of a gnat
gives me eight hand-written pages he wants me to read
his silly mother is there presiding over funeral arrangements
in this dream neither paul drowns
not in the lake one august afternoon
nor in the hospital with somebody
else's liver sewn inside
i'm going to be a writer says the boy
he jingles his keys

flowers sprout the third night where there was never a garden
i plan a poetry lesson teach them flower-writing how to draw
without looking how to make their colours from scratch we're
outside with creeks interspersed and snake grass underfoot
                                                    a tsunami
washes over everything the notebooks and pencils the babies are lost
from their mothers the fathers from their sons and vice versa in the calm
aftermath i'm in the kindergarten where a microwave is a tv
                                        is a washing machine
by the end we're sitting on the floor in the play house
each of us watching a different channel
from the same little wooden box

later that same century
after Czeslaw Milosz's "Rising of the Sun"

i didn't support the treaty of versailles didn't load the slave
ships off the gold coast was neither for nor against the confederates
in the civil war i have no ships bombs or guns the day i was born
airplanes full of people flew over a sea a continent the last circus
creaked through town when i was twenty-eight and nets came up
heavy with cod off the grand banks the heartbeat of ages before me
was the rosy sun rising and setting the luminous eye of the moon
winking and blinking and so it will be in ages to come

i was not yet conceived when the ovens of treblinka consumed
the flesh of jews when the wide ravines of latvian towns were filled
with murdered mothers fathers their children not yet born when
the bombs exploded over hiroshima and nagasaki later that same
century jane and i made pine needle salad served fern frond fish
and stone potatoes on cracked 78 records our home a broken-
down boat atop grassy waves always cresting never breaking
and we rode wild green horses down the lane as far as the mud
daubers and back
                        one day their prickly rumps transmogrified into
the drooping boughs of norway spruce   stones became stones
potatoes potatoes

                                        at the dawning
as they say of the new millennium it's nine o'clock i stand
before a room full of children arranged in rows sing o canada
alone why won't you sing i ask the music is too high or too low
they say they are shy i cannot make them sing i teach them
the difference between colons and semi-colons tell them if you
write a letter to the prime minister he will answer you don't
need a stamp i explain this history is a story somebody makes
up we musn't call them indians

                        o where do you come from sadie
and taylor where are you going do you have a plan jordan do you
believe you will know when something is right or wrong and sameera
my love will you eat the flesh of the stories or my dears my dears will
you just nod off to sleep

deer stories

1

four-year-old kate and her dog buddy
cross the empty field north of the house
buddy runs ahead into the woods and out
                                    leaps a deer
like a sharp intake of breath the young doe stands
on the freshly-harrowed earth
                              then turns
leaps over the neighbour's fence
                              and is gone

a smaller deer lunges into the open
but kate doesn't see
she is practising her princess walk
with both hands she lifts the hem
of her vegetable garden dress
the one i love with the radishes
the yellow-handled shovels, the carrots
and eggplant

she steps daintily
places her feet just so
              here and here and
                              here

the deer sails over her head
and crosses the field
raising small poofs of dust
where its hoofs touch down

2.

the hottest night of the year
and in spite of lake huron
                            no breeze
to dance relief across our skin
all the children but one—the oldest—
are asleep
            submerged
in the muggy air
of a canvas tent
my friend and i—desperate from the heat—
promise   *we won't be long*
leave our only flashlight behind so he can keep watch

our tent, pitched near the beach
is a quick walk in daylight through to the lake
but in this dark we follow the path slowly between
juniper-laced dunes
                    clumps of poison ivy

our plan: to swim

we take small steps
faces down-turned

            crackle of dry brush
                                        something large
to our left
            we hold still
                            wait
just a little afraid

a doe steps out of the moonless dark
onto the trail in front of us
i've never been so close to a wild animal

i reach out
touch her flank
her fur is wet
soaked in sweat
she crosses the trail ahead
                    returns to the dark

i wonder why she didn't flinch
when i touched her
how she knew and didn't know
something was
and wasn't
            happening

3.

my youngest sister and i walk
on a path through spring woods
it's raining a little
our children run ahead
back when i was thirteen and she was three
i was always holding her hand
pushing her on swings   catching her
at the bottom of slides
i picked her up and carried her home the time she tripped
and fell on her face in the kipling heights plaza parking lot
knocked out three of her front teeth

over the years
                i watched her marriage fall apart
her single parenting
                        the shifting
careers
        the fumbling
the trying to make a go of it, i witnessed
from a place i occupied with our father and other gods
whose hollowed-be-thy-names are
                as i discovered last year after my own divorce
full of shit.

we two follow the path
around a stand of birch and o

                        a deer

the stillness

she looks directly at us
                    sees us

her alertness
            kinetic—

energy sizzles in
the light rain

4.

i've seen many deer since
                        on the run
                                in the air
over
            brush piles
                                fences

fleeing
            down or up
steep slopes
                along ridges

the other day at the art gallery
i turned the corner of one more white room
found a deer giving birth to a full-grown woman

the woman's feet were folded together
                                    inside

the rest of her
                stretched out
on the white carpeted floor
arms bent at the elbow
hands held close
to her face
she looked startled
                thoughtful

the fingers of one hand touching her lips

was she choosing not to speak
or was she considering her words

i know what it is
to be born from a deer

surprised
            and wondering
how will i tell *this* story

why the gully is never lonely

my sister jennifer and her daughter kate of the famous eggplant
and red wheelbarrow dress sing *dona nobis pacem* in two parts
on the edge of the gully it's a warm day in early april the skunk
cabbage not quite unfurled

                              from where i sit on a crumbling log
their backs are to me and they sing out over the collapse
of a thousand or more years and everything with ears hears them
and everything without ears feels the unheard-of vibrations

                              do the leaves sigh and settle deeper
into their demise are the trees soothed by the gentle pulsations
from the strings in two human throats thickening and tightening
lengthening and loosening the gently rhythmic waves emanating
from their open mouths
                              kate sings another song
a solo every musical syllable a pebble every word a handful
 of pebbles tossed into the gully-complicated air we stand
in silence knowing *ave maria* has made countless circles
that go out forever bumping into other circles made by birds
and cracks of thunder and explosions even the sobbing and
hopeless pleading that millions have made for mercy over time

the rain begins and we head back to our island shelter
of white pine and sumac   eat rice cakes and cheese
split our one orange three ways

the secret way to sauble beach

one summer morning
when my first son was a baby
i packed him into his car seat
behind me and drove north
up the peninsula to port elgin
he cried off and on all the way
later that night it was me behind him
his head bigger than the moon, his chubby heels
sunk deep into the pebble beach

twenty-five years later he calls me up
to read me part of a hart crane poem
just a few lines he promises
because i love it he says
                       i love it so much

tomorrow he'll load a ford 350
diesel with pumps and pipe
drive it up to beaverdell
northeast of vancouver

he reads and reads
says he's sorry
there's just a little more
i lean back
close my eyes

before my son had words i drove him crying
through clandeboyne, the secret way to sauble beach
one summer weekend so he would tell me
what he loves and it is poetry

black-crowned night heron

southeast of sparta at nightfall
i spot it lying near the road
not sure it's dead
no blood
no twisted bone or crushed part
just green feet
feathers chocolate-brown
stippled white at the tips
slate-gray
nearest the skin
an aggressive grey
surprisingly serious for a colour

i carry it away from the gravelly shoulder
lay it down between the soybean field
and the trickling creek that was its home
pluck handfuls of grass
arrange them over the body
breathe a small prayer without words

later i mention the incident to my cousin
collector of butterflies and raccoon skins
there's a guy out near belmont she says
you've seen the place
charlie's cheese and taxidermy

i wonder about fame
and books of poetry going on without me
this writing to preserve in books
                              hush
                              of the heron
                              crossing the road at dusk

 hush of the woman composing a line that sings

isn't that what we long to keep
the flying out, the flying
out at dusk

74

not the heaven of raccoons

philosophically and logistically speaking
there are some problems with my theory
of separate heavens for separate people
as my sister pointed out the other night
when we met for coffee after going to
the funeral home

wouldn't it be lonely she wondered

my response involves advanced theories of quantum physics
in which the universe is expanding so fast that there are infinite
alternate universes created which are almost identical to other
universes except that in one universe there might be raccoons up
in trees while hound dogs bark underneath them and in another
universe the raccoons are in the cornfield feasting while in heaven
right next door somebody has plugged a radio into a long extension
cord and music from the local radio station has scared the raccoons
away and bushels of corn are picked by a woman who loves the feel
of the perfect ears in her hands because this is her heaven you see
not the heaven of raccoons

acknowledgements

thanks to John Buschek of BuschekBooks

many thanks to the magazines and anthologies where many of these poems first appeared: *Canadian Forum, Grain, The New Quarterly, Room of One's Own, Carousel, The Literary Review of Canada, Henry's Creature* (Black Moss Press, 2000), *following the plough; recovering the rural* Black Moss Press, 2000), *Open Wide a Wilderness* (Wilfred Laurier Press, 2009)

"an immense indiscernible shift is going on in the world" and "to be the teacher" won first and third prize in the short Grain contest in 2005.

i would like to thank the Ontario Arts Council for generous funding through the Writers' Reserve Program, and the editors of the many publications who recommended me

a special thanks to the members of my London, Ontario writing group for their on-going encouragement and sage advice in matters of the word and of the heart

my gratitude to Sheila Stewart for reading many of the poems and offering suggestions

and thank you to Cornelia Hoogland who accompanied me to the birthplace of the gully and back

my deep appreciation for the Banff Centre for the Arts and the 2008 Writing Studio which allowed for 5 weeks of poetry—writing, thinking, talking, eating poetry, and the inspiration, advice and guidance of John Steffler, Mary Dalton and Don McKay.

and my gratitude to jonathan for the love, the support and the understanding, not to mention the sturdiness of the porch on hincks and the immaculate moldings inside